Bonjour, là, Bonjour

BONJOUR LA BONJOUR

A Play by Michel Tremblay
Translated by John Van Burek & Bill Glassco
Talonbooks, Vancouver, 1975

published with assistance from the Canada Council

Talonbooks
201 1019 East Cordova
Vancouver
British Columbia V6A 1M8
Canada

This book was typeset by Linda Gilbert at B.C. Monthly Typesetting Service and designed by A.A. Bronson with David Robinson for Talonbooks.

The back cover photograph was taken by François Brunelle.

First printing: December 1975

Talonplays are edited by Peter Hay.

First published by Les Editions Leméac Inc., Montréal, Québec. Published by arrangement with Les Editions Leméac Inc.

ISBN 0-88922-091-3

Bonjour, là, Bonjour was first performed by the Compagnie des Deux Chaises at the National Art Centre in Ottawa, Ontario, on August 22, 1974, with the following cast:

Lucienne	Denise Pelletier
Denise	Amulette Garneau
Monique	Monique Joly
Nicole	Odette Gagnon
Albertine	Rita Lafontaine
Charlotte	Frédérique Collin
Gabriel	Gilles Renaud
Serge	Guy Thauvette

Directed by André Brassard
Designed by Guy Neveu
Costumes by François Laplante

Bonjour, là, Bonjour was first performed in English at Tarragon Theatre in Toronto, Ontario, on February 1, 1975, with the following cast:

Lucienne	Patricia Hamilton
Denise	Janet Amos
Monique	Samantha Langevin
Nicole	Diana Leblanc
Albertine	Helen Hughes
Charlotte	Doris Petrie
Gabriel	Ed McNamara
Serge	Jim Henshaw

Directed by Bill Glassco
Designed by Grant Guy
Lighting by Vladimir Svetlovsky

No. 1 Trio

GABRIEL:
So, how did you like Europe?

ALBERTINE:
Your aunt would have loved that, to go away on trips.

CHARLOTTE:
You know what your aunt's always dreamed of? To take a trip around the world.

GABRIEL:
Is it as nice as everyone says?

ALBERTINE
AND CHARLOTTE:
But no, your aunt was never that lucky.

GABRIEL:
You're a lucky fellow, you know that? You're the first one in the family to cross the Atlantic.

ALBERTINE:
No he's not . . .

GABRIEL:
Oh yeah, your uncle Fernand during the war, but when he got there it was all over. They just turned him around and shipped him back.

CHARLOTTE:
No, your aunt was never that lucky.

GABRIEL:
He never got past London and that's only in England. Never had time. Nope, you're the first.

ALBERTINE:
Were you sick to your stomach on the plane?

GABRIEL:
That's what I was telling the boys at the tavern the other day. I said, "My Serge is the first one in the family to spend three whole months in Europe."

CHARLOTE:
Three months . . . Well, your aunt could spend three years far from this place.

GABRIEL:
I bought them a round and I told them everything you said in your letters. Oh they probably heard it before, but when I buy, they listen. They know what I've got to say is important, even if they heard it before . . . And if any of them don't want to listen, Bonnier just tells them to shut up and he goes over and turns off the television. So I stood up and I told them everything you said in your letters from Greece.

ALBERTINE:
That must be long, eh, seven hours on the plane?

CHARLOTTE:
They say Paris is shaped like an onion. Is that really true?

GABRIEL:

You should have seen the look on their faces. Oh they're a nice bunch of guys alright, but they don't know anything. They've never been further than Guy and Dorchester. You mention St-Lambert, they don't know what you're talking about. And there's a couple of young snots in there too who don't want to believe me. Seems they started shouting, "Water that blue? Impossible! Sit down, Gabriel, you're making it all up." Of course me, I couldn't hear them. Well, all Bonnier had to do was show them the stamp on the envelope and that shut them up fast!

CHARLOTTE:

Be honest now, is the water really that blue?

ALBERTINE:

Now Charlotte, if Serge said so . . .

GABRIEL:

They're just jealous, the whole bunch of 'em. They've never done a thing since the day they were born and they probably never will. Of course when it's time to criticize, they know everything. That's for sure. Even when it isn't time. Oh they loaf around the tavern all day, make fun of everyone else, but you think they'd lift a finger to go out and earn some money? Not on your life. I tell those young buggers all the time, and you know me, I don't mince words. "You're not even twenty-five," I tell them, "and here you are acting like me, a retired man. Is this what you call the future generation of tomorrow? Come on, get off your asses! You go on like this, you won't amount to a thing. You go on like this, you won't even get a wife. And those of you who got a wife, I sure hope you buy some life-savers before you go home, because you smell like a cow." You know what one of them said to me once? He screamed it right in my face to make sure I'd understand. "Me," he says, "I drink my beer here and the old lady drinks hers at home. So we got no problem with bad breath." At times like that I'm sorry I can read lips . . .

ALBERTINE:
> That must be quite a change, eh, to live in a different country with people you don't even know?

CHARLOTTE:
> Of course silly old me, every morning I'd go downstairs to see if there wasn't a letter.

ALBERTINE:
> It must be hard to get used to, eh?

CHARLOTTE:
> As if you had time to write every day! You don't even phone us when you're here so why would you write every day from Europe?

ALBERTINE:
> You're gonna laugh, but you know something? Everytime they showed a French movie on television, I thought of you. And I'd ask myself, "How in the world does he do it?"

CHARLOTTE:
> Your father got pretty worried sometimes when we hadn't heard for a while . . .

GABRIEL:
> But here I am doing all the talking and you're the one who's just come home . . .

CHARLOTTE:
> Your father got pretty worried sometimes when we hadn't heard for a while . . .

ALBERTINE:
> Alright, Charlotte, once was enough!

CHARLOTTE:
> Well, he wasn't listening! Nobody ever listens to me.

ALBERTINE:
>   If nobody listens to you it's because you're a bore.

CHARLOTTE:
>   And what makes you think you're so interesting?

GABRIEL:
>   Are the European girls pretty?

ALBERTINE
AND CHARLOTTE:
>   Are the European girls pretty?

ALBERTINE:
>   We thought you might come home with a girl from Paris.

CHARLOTTE:
>   Oh, that would have surprised me . . .

ALBERTINE:
>   So that would have surprised you, would it?

CHARLOTTE:
>   Of course it would.

ALBERTINE:
>   And why, might I ask?

CHARLOTTE:
>   I've got my reasons . . .

ALBERTINE:
>   Well, aren't you the clever one . . .

CHARLOTTE:
>   Look, I've got my reasons!

ALBERTINE:
>   Always a bit smarter than the rest of us, aren't you?

CHARLOTTE:
> I didn't say I was smarter. I said it would have surprised me, that's all.

ALBERTINE:
> Well, you're probably right. Serge has better taste than that.

GABRIEL:
> I knew one once. Oh that was a long time ago, before your mother. A Belgian girl. That was way back in the twenties. In those days there weren't so many immigrants as they got now. She wasn't all that pretty, but she was interesting to talk to. That was a long time before . . . My accident. I never would have married her though. Oh no! I don't know how they do it, those people who marry foreigners. But you know, she used to tell me about all the trouble they had over there. It's hard to believe, eh? War, famine . . . Everything's happened to those poor people. They've been through it all. You know, when you stop to think about it, we've got no right to complain. Over here, we've got it good.

CHARLOTTE:
> Not that good!

GABRIEL:
> Mind you, that was a long time ago. Maybe things are better now.

ALBERTINE:
> How come you don't eat? Your plate's been sitting there for five minutes. You haven't even touched it . . . I thought you liked roast beef.

CHARLOTTE:
> Maybe it's too rare. He likes it well done, you know.

ALBERTINE:
> That's right too. I forgot you liked the outside. Goodness me, the things you forget in three months . . .

CHARLOTTE:
>Would you like Aunt Charlotte to change your plate?
>Here, I'll get you some more peas too.

ALBERTINE:
>Maybe I should warm up the potatoes . . .

GABRIEL:
>Don't be afraid to tell me about Paris. Oh I know I've
>never been there, but I've read a lot. I've read all about
>that stuff. I got the whole map of Paris right here in the
>old noggin. Your old man's not stupid you know.
>Maybe I've never been past Guy and Dorchester either,
>but at least I've read up on these things. You know the
>Eiffel Tower? I can tell you where it is. It's on the
>Left Bank. And Notre Dame, I know where that is too.
>It's on the Ile de la Cité. Victor Hugo talked so much
>about that in his book. You know, when I was out of
>work during the Depression, I used to read all kinds of
>things. You wouldn't remember that 'cause you weren't
>born then, but ask Lucienne. Maupassant and all those
>things. I read them all.

ALBERTINE:
>Maybe he's tired. Maybe he doesn't want to tell us
>everything now.

GABRIEL:
>What?

ALBERTINE: *louder*
>I said, maybe he's tired. He can tell us about it another
>time.

GABRIEL:
>To hell! A son's too tired to talk to his father? We
>haven't seen each other for three months. We got such
>an earful about this trip before he left. Don't tell me he's
>got nothing to say now that he's back. Besides, you told
>me yourself at Dorval that because of that time change,

you've got to stay awake at least until midnight. So go ahead, shoot, I'm listening.

ALBERTINE:
Let him eat, Gabriel, he can tell us about it later.

No. 2 Duet

SERGE: *too loudly, articulating too much for his father to understand him* Paris is really beautiful! It's a . . . fabulous city. It's big. Er . . . Wherever you go it's beautiful. I mean, there are no ugly places. At least I didn't see any.

Louder.

I said I didn't see any place in Paris that wasn't beautiful. And it's true, the Seine . . . it's not very wide.

Trying to be funny.

It looks more like a duck pond than a river . . .

Silence.

Er . . . When it's all lit up at night, you know, the Louvre and all that, it's unbelievable. I thought about you a lot when I was out walking.

Louder.

I said, I thought about you when I was out walking, how you love to take walks. And I knew you'd have liked it there. You don't realize it at the time, but you walk for hours and hours. You never get bored. There's always something interesting to see. What's really fun is to see the names of streets because it reminds you of so many things. Books, movies, songs . . . And even the street corners are nice 'cause they aren't at right angles like they are here. There are always five or six streets that come together in the same place so sometimes the streets don't even have corners.

ALBERTINE:

I don't think he hears you, Serge. His hearing aid is broken. He's too proud to tell you.

No. 3 Octet

We can hear LUCIENNE laughing before the lights come up on her. The actress should bear in mind that in the original, LUCIENNE speaks French with a slight English accent as though she has lost the habit of speaking her mother tongue.

LUCIENNE:

Well, if nothing else, did they show you how to live. My God, with hair that long . . . I guess you haven't changed much. Come on, why don't you get that cut? It's not even in style anymore. Even Bobby gets his cut now and he's only sixteen.

SERGE:

How is Bobby? Still the family bum?

CHARLOTTE:

Lucienne phoned. She wants you to go and see her.

ALBERTINE:

She spoke to your Aunt Charlotte. Didn't even ask how I was.

LUCIENNE:

> Bobby? Oh his father's right, he'll straighten out. It's his age. Kids always do crazy things at his age. He'll be alright.

SERGE:

> And the girl he knocked up, will she be alright too?

LUCIENNE:

> Look, if you've come here to talk about that again . . . I don't need you to bring up my kids.

SERGE:

> Lucienne, I came because you asked me to.

LUCIENNE:

> And you wouldn't have come if I hadn't?

SERGE:

> No, I wouldn't.

LUCIENNE:

> Then why did you bother?

SERGE:

> I thought it might be important since you took the trouble to phone me at Papa's . . .

LUCIENNE:

> I didn't want you running straight to Nicole's. We'd never see you again.

> *MONIQUE appears.*

MONIQUE:

> Hi there, lover boy! You finally made it, eh? I've only been waiting for two hours. Hey, before you take off your coat, will you go to the drugstore for me?

LUCIENNE:

> Are you moving back to her place?

SERGE:

Her place is my place.

NICOLE tries to say something but without success.

LUCIENNE:

Hey, turn off the stereo, it's giving me a headache. I want to talk to you . . . seriously. The first button on the left . . . It's new, did you notice? No, of course not, you never notice things like that . . .

SERGE:

What do you mean? Of course I noticed . . .

LUCIENNE:

Well, you might have said something. It cost me a thousand bucks.

SERGE:

Look, I'm not a kid anymore. Don't expect me to do handstands every time you buy a salad bowl. I noticed your new bar too, but I didn't say anything 'cause I think a bar in the corner of a living room is really ugly and yours is especially God awful.

LUCIENNE:

You're getting jealous . . . just like the others . . .

DENISE appears.

DENISE:

Well, well, well, what a surprise! Come on in! Guess what, I've got a roast beef in the oven. How's that grab you? Here, give us a kiss, a nice big juicy kiss.

SERGE:

Look, if you're going to start that again, I'm going home to bed. I'm too tired . . .

LUCIENNE:

> No, no, stay here. Stay. Stay the night if you like. You can sleep in the guest room. You know it's been refurnished, eh, since you left? I got tired of the Colonial. It looked cheap . . .

SERGE:

> I'm the one who told you that . . .

LUCIENNE:

> So we bought a set of Spanish. It's gorgeous.

> *Silence.*

> You're gonna love it. We put the Colonial in the basement for Bobby and his friends.

> *Silence.*

> So, you had a good trip. Tell me all about it . . .

MONIQUE:

> How much do I owe you?

SERGE:

> Forget it . . .

MONIQUE:

> Don't be silly, you're not going to pay for my pills. Wow . . . They're a lot more expensive than I thought . . . I can't afford these too often . . .

LUCIENNE:

> I suppose you've just told Papa about it and you don't fell like starting all over . . .

SERGE:

> Lucienne, have you forgotten how we parted three months ago?

18

LUCIENNE:

    So that's it . . . You're still mad at me.

MONIQUE:

    And there's only twelve of them! They must be kidding.

LUCIENNE:

    Even after three months . . .

MONIQUE:

    Bob told me I'd have enough for a month!

SERGE:

    Maybe you're not supposed to take them every day . . .

LUCIENNE:

    Okay, so I got a little drunk that night . . . and you don't like it when people get drunk.

SERGE:

    I don't mind if people drink provided they don't bawl me out and provided they don't throw up all over my plate.

LUCIENNE:

    Serge, I don't remember everything I did, but I certainly did not throw up all over your plate.

SERGE:

    Okay, okay, let's not get into that tonight . . . I've got other people to see . . .

MONIQUE:

    If things keep going the way they are, I'll take the whole bottle, and then . . .

SERGE:

    So long.

MONIQUE:

    So long everybody.

19

LUCIENNE:

> Look, I asked you to stay . . . I have something important to tell you.

ALBERTINE
AND CHARLOTTE:

> Your father ran into your sister Lucienne on la rue Ste-Catherine the other day . . .

GABRIEL:

> I ran into your sister Lucienne on la rue St-Catherine the other day . . .

ALBERTINE
AND CHARLOTTE:

> Your father ran into your sister Lucienne on la rue Ste-Catherine the other day and . . .

SERGE:

> Okay, what is it this time?

ALBERTINE
AND CHARLOTTE:

> She was with another man . . .

MONIQUE:

> For a while I stopped taking them altogether . . . I felt better too. But now . . . now I get these funny feelings . . .

LUCIENNE:

> I know it sounds funny . . .

DENISE:

> It's funny. I'd forgotten you were so tall.

MONIQUE:

> I'm so feverish lately . . .

DENISE:
>But then it must be those stupid shoes, eh, with the thick soles . . .

MONIQUE:
>At times, you know, I feel fine, then all of a sudden I get dizzy. I can't see straight. It really scares me . . .

DENISE:
>Holy cow, little brother, are you good looking!

MONIQUE:
>It was Bob who gave me the prescription. It's supposed to be strong, but he says it works wonders.

DENISE:
>Come on, sexy, don't stand there in the door. Come in and sit down. You're giving me hot flashes!

>*NICOLE tries again to say something but without success.*

LUCIENNE:
>You know that things aren't too hot between Bob and me. We've been married for twenty years . . . Well, we know all about that. Bonjour, bonjour. Bonsoir, bonsoir. That's about it. Small talk, you know what I mean?

SERGE:
>Nothing new about that.

LUCIENNE:
>Well . . . I've met someone else . . .

SERGE:
>That's fine.

LUCIENNE:
>Is that all you can say?

SERGE:

>If you're happy, I'm happy for you.

LUCIENNE:

>There's one problem . . .

SERGE:

>I figured as much.

LUCIENNE:

>Will you listen to me . . . Will you let me explain? It's not easy to say . . .

ALBERTINE
AND CHARLOTTE:

>Some young fella . . .

LUCIENNE:

>He's your age . . .

ALBERTINE:

>It's disgusting. A mother with a family!

CHARLOTTE:

>That's what you call a pig!

GABRIEL:

>I pretended not to see her. I didn't want to embarrass her. But I think she saw me. As she walked by, she looked in a store window. I think you know him too . . .

LUCIENNE:

>And you know him.

SERGE:

>I even know him! Hey, this story's getting better all the time. When you tell me his name, I suppose I'll jump up and say, "Not him, it can't be him!"

GABRIEL:
>It's that tall guy you used to bring home all the time . . .
>You know, the one who looked like you . . . The painter.
>Always smelled like Varsol . . .

SERGE:
>Robert?
>
>*Laughing.*
>
>Not him, it can't be him!

LUCIENNE:
>It's your friend Robert.

SERGE:
>I know.

LUCIENNE:
>So Papa did see me on the street the other day?

SERGE:
>Yep!

LUCIENNE:
>Shit! Shit! Shit! Shit! . . . What are you laughing at?

SERGE:
>You're married to a Bob, you've got a kid named Bobby
>and out of all my friends you had to go and fall for one
>named Robert.

LUCIENNE:
>Sure, to you it's only a joke.

DENISE:
>If I don't control myself, I'm gonna rape you on the
>spot.

SERGE:
>Then control yourself.

DENISE:

> After three months? When I dream about you every night?

SERGE:

> Here Denise, have some peanuts.

LUCIENNE:

> That's all you've got to say?

SERGE:

> Look, I don't care about your sordid affairs. Sleep with whoever you like. If it thaws you out a bit, so much the better.

LUCIENNE:

> This is not sordid. It's serious.

SERGE:

> Oh for Chrissake, open your eyes. That's Robert's specialty, shacking up with women who could pass for his mother. Whatever happens, don't take him seriously. Have your fun and when it's over, forget him. Just don't make a Greek tragedy out of it. I'm not in the mood.

DENISE
AND MONIQUE:

> Have you been to Lady Westmount's?

LUCIENNE:

> How dare you talk to me like that. I won't have it! I'm the one who brought you up and . . .

SERGE:

> Lucienne, please! If you asked me to come here it's because you want someone to talk to, anyone, and it's not because you brought me up that . . .

LUCIENNE:

Okay, but can't you see, I don't know what to do anymore?

SERGE:

Don't play games with me. You're supposed to be the smart one in the family, the tough one, the one who's made it. You're trying to tell me you don't know what to do? You're telling me you want to drop everything for Robert? Come on! You'd never leave all this to go hole-up in a basement with a guy who stinks of paint. I know you better than that. Look, you're married to a doctor, an Anglais on top of that, you've got a seventy thousand dollar house in Cartierville, a charming son who's started to knock up the neighbourhood girls, and two lovely teenage twins who flatly refuse to learn French because their father speaks nothing but English. Now how could you leave all that, Lucienne? You love it too much.

DENISE:

Is Lady Westmount still unhappy, even with all her money?

MONIQUE:

Does she still have her rich-lady problems?

DENISE
AND MONIQUE:

Did she manage to make you feel sorry for her?

NICOLE:

Are you going to come back and stay with me?

> *SERGE throws himself into NICOLE's arms. They embrace for a long time.*

SERGE:

Yes! . . . Yes! . . . Yes!

NICOLE:

I missed you so much.

SERGE:

Me too . . .

DENISE:

Why don't you take a shower, sexy? You can walk around in your underpants, I'll lose weight just looking at you.

LUCIENNE:

I thought you'd help me think this out, but no, you sit there and laugh at me.

NICOLE and SERGE separate.

DENISE:

Okay, enough of this nonsense. Down to serious business. Come on little brother, let's eat. It's awful, you know, I'm getting to be such a pig. Every year it gets worse.

SERGE:

Where's Gaston? Isn't he home?

DENISE:

His bowling, dear, have you forgotten his bowling? My life still depends on his gutter balls, no kidding. It's been that way for fifteen years. Come on, I've got boiled potatoes or baked potatoes. What's your preference?

SERGE:

I'm not hungry, I already ate at Papa's.

DENISE:

Why didn't you wait to eat here? Albertine can't cook to save her life. Especially a roast. The last time I went there for supper I could have used an axe.

LUCIENNE:

Listen to me, dammit!

DENISE:

Is that what you had, roast beef?

SERGE:

Yes . . .

DENISE:

And didn't you need an axe?

SERGE:

It would have helped . . .

DENISE:

Well, there you are . . .

SERGE:

But what difference does it make?

DENISE:

What difference does it make? Don't you care about eating?

MONIQUE:

It all came back to me while you were gone, Serge, everything I'd been scared of . . . I thought it was over and done with, but . . .

SERGE:

Did you tell your husband about it?

MONIQUE:

I didn't tell anyone. I don't want them to put me away.

SERGE:

They're not going to put you away . . .

MONIQUE:
> That's what you think. They watch me all the time.
> Sometimes in the morning, when I'm not feeling well,
> you should see the look on their faces. They're just
> waiting for me to crack.

SERGE:
> You'd solve half the problem if you'd get rid of your
> mother-in-law. I've told you that a hundred times.

LUCIENNE:
> I want you to listen!

DENISE:
> Not even a little slice of well done? It's the outside, you
> know. Your favourite . . . No? You sure?

No. 4 Quartet

LUCIENNE:
> It's true, I've got everything I ever dreamed of. I told
> myself I wasn't going to end up like Mama, with nothing.
> I made sure that wouldn't happen to me.

SERGE:
> Here we go again, Lucienne in "The Edge of Night".

MONIQUE:
> Did Lady Westmount start on Mama again?

LUCIENNE:
> I wasn't going to marry some French-Canadian turd
> who'd give me kids with complexes. Oh no, I was aiming
> higher than that. I wanted to be on the right side of
> the tracks, the money side, and that's where I am,
> dammit.

DENISE:
> To complain like that on a full stomach. It's amost
> indecent.

LUCIENNE:

    I got what I wanted, I got my Anglais. Eight years I went out with Bob before we got married.

SERGE:

    Yeah, yeah, we know all that . . .

LUCIENNE:

    I made up my mind I was going to marry him and I did. If I had to wait till he finished school and set up his office, then I'd wait.

DENISE:

    She's been going on like that for months. It's ridiculous . . . She must have nothing else to do . . .

LUCIENNE:

    When we went out together, I paid because I was earning the money. But I didn't care. I didn't care because I knew that someday he'd pay it all back, that he'd pay me back even more than that. Because I knew that someday he'd be making big money!

SERGE:

    Yeah, yeah, sure . . .

LUCIENNE:

    Well, my God, big money isn't the word for it . . . As for kids, I wanted two but we had three. The only mistake in our whole life. Instead of having one child the second time, we had two.

MONIQUE:

    And her twins, are they still nervous wrecks?

DENISE:

    Did you see the little monsters?

LUCIENNE:

    Everything else in our life is exactly the way we planned it.

SERGE
AND LUCIENNE:

> We started out at the bottom of the ladder and we climbed, step by step . . .

LUCIENNE:

> It took us twenty years, but our dreams have all come true. How do you like that, eh? Well, kiddo, if you only knew. I'm not even forty-five and already my life works just like a clock. And that's what they call "having your dreams come true."

DENISE:

> The last time I called her she told me she felt like a clock or something like that . . . She's off her rocker, that one . . .

MONIQUE:

> And people tell me I'm off my rocker!

LUCIENNE:

> It gets to the point there's nothing left to do. You sit there day in and day out while your life goes on by itself without you and you don't know what to do. To pass the time you go out and buy things, then you stick them in the basement because they're too big . . . Or you sit and watch your kids grow up. Me, I couldn't care less about watching my kids grow up. I'm not interested in children. I never have been.

MONIQUE:

> With a doctor for a husband she could have all the pills she wants . . .

LUCIENNE:

> I don't know, sometimes I wonder if I even love my kids. But what's the difference, they love their father more than they do me. He's the hero. He's the one who started out with nothing, he's the one who's made it. Not me. Well, I've got . . . what, twenty-five, thirty

years left to live? And already I know everything that's going to happen to me.

SERGE:

So to fight the boredom you run after young studs . . .

LUCIENNE:

You're so stupid, so stupid. My God, are you stupid!

No. 5 Octet

SERGE:

Lucienne, how many times have we been through this routine? How many times have you asked me to come all the way out here because you had something important to tell me when all you really want to tell me is how boring your life is and why I should feel sorry for you? Well, find something to do if you're so bored. Okay, granted, you've found something to do, but let me tell you this, going to bed with my friend Robert is not going to solve your problems. He's the dullest guy I ever met.

ALBERTINE:

I still can't get over it . . .

SERGE:

And don't start telling me you're in love with him, either.

ALBERTINE:

A girl in her position . . .

SERGE:

You can fuck yourselves black and blue for all I care. Just cut the soap opera.

LUCIENNE:
Look, I've told you, I won't have that language in my house.

SERGE:
Oh, the doctor's wife is still with us . . .

CHARLOTTE:
A doctor's wife . . .

GABRIEL:
But what in the world is wrong with her?

SERGE: *laughing*
Oh, that . . .

MONIQUE:
The last time I went to see Bob, he almost laughed in my face. You know what he told me? To take my pills and stop thinking.

SERGE:
Go see someone else . . .

ALBERTINE:
That must be why she doesn't phone us anymore. She's too ashamed. And your poor father, he's aged ten years since he saw her with that bum. No. If you're a lady, you should act like a lady!

GABRIEL:
I can't believe she'd ruin her life for nothing. She's worked so hard.

SERGE:
Don't worry, Papa.

Louder.

I said, don't worry. It's not that serious!

GABRIEL:

    Are you going to go and see her?

SERGE:

    It won't do any good . . .

GABRIEL:

    Of course it will! I can't go, she won't listen to me.
    She thinks I'm stupid. But you, she'll listen to you.

CHARLOTTE:

    You'd think that would have occurred to her, eh? I
    mean, if she's going to do that with one of your friends,
    you'd be sure to find out sooner or later.

DENISE:

    Hey, little brother, you know what you should do, you
    should come and live with us. Look at you. You're
    skinny as a rail. Your loving sister doesn't feed you
    enough. Or was it those Frenchies tried to starve you
    to death? Seriously, you could have the front parlour,
    we never use it. There's loads of room. You wouldn't
    have to worry about us, you could come and go as you
    please. And me . . . I'd spoil you rotten . . .

SERGE:

    Sure, Denise. Have you told Gaston about your little
    project?

DENISE:

    Gaston? Who's Gaston?

LUCIENNE:

    I think I have the right to a little respect in my own
    house.

DENISE:

    As if Gaston ever once made a decision in his life!

NICOLE:

    You went to see the others first, didn't you?

ALBERTINE:

>All this excitement, it's not good for your father . . .
>His heart can't take it . . .

CHARLOTTE:

>His heart can't stand the strain . . .

NICOLE:

>I'm sorry, that was stupid, what I just said. I should
>know better. You just walked in the door . . . Well . . .
>Take off your coat.

DENISE:

>You mean I have to eat it all by myself? The whole
>roast beef? You'll help me with dessert though, eh? A
>nice piece of mincemeat pie . . .

SERGE:

>You know my soft spot, don't you?

DENISE:

>You bet I do!

NICOLE:

>Anyway, I think I know why you came here last . . .

SERGE smiles at NICOLE.

CHARLOTTE:

>There's Nicole too, we're worried about her . . .

SERGE:

>You're always worried about something, aren't you?

ALBERTINE:

>Well, naturally, we're concerned about all of you . . .
>Ever since your mother died, we're the ones . . .

SERGE:
>Aunt Bartine, that was ten years ago. I'm not fifteen anymore, I'm twenty-five and I'm the youngest in the family. We're old enough to take care of ourselves, thank you.

CHARLOTTE:
>If we can't even open our mouths . . .

ALBERTINE:
>How dare you talk to me like that! . . . You have no right . . .

MONIQUE:
>By the way, thanks for sending all your postcards to the wrong address. It's nice to know that Madame Proulx downstairs knows more about you than your own sister.

NICOLE:
>It's funny. I just got your last letter this morning . . .

DENISE:
>It's a good thing you didn't write me any letters. It took me three days just to figure out your postcards.

SERGE:
>The one where I told you that after three months I finally decided to go see the Louvre?

NICOLE:
>No . . . No . . . I didn't get that one yet . . .

DENISE:
>Speaking of postcards, you know those bridges? Are they right in the middle of the city or all around it like the bridges in Montreal?

SERGE:
>They're in the middle of the city . . .

DENISE:
Wouldn't you know it, Gaston was right.

NICOLE:
That means there's one that hasn't come yet. That'll be fun, we can read it together . . .

GABRIEL:
I've got that headache again . . . Hey, Bartine, you got any aspirin?

ALBERTINE:
I don't like it when he gets these headaches.

CHARLOTTE:
That's three days in a row now . . . It must be the excitement, what with you coming home . . .

SERGE: *very loudly*
Is it any better? Your hearing, is it getting any better?

GABRIEL:
Ah, don't talk about that . . . Forget it . . . Forget it.

DENISE:
So that means Paris isn't on an island . . .

MONIQUE:
I called home yesterday and Aunt Charlotte answered the phone . . . I thought it was yesterday you were coming back. Aren't they depressing, those two? I'm so sick of hearing about their health all the time.

LUCIENNE:
Well, say something!

SERGE:
You're twenty years older than me, I have no advice to give you.

No. 6 Duet

NICOLE:
It's like . . . it's like waking up after a bad dream. Or as if I'd been locked up somewhere for years without seeing a soul. Before you left, we said that while you were gone we'd think everything over, but the minute you got on the plane, I knew it was all thought out in advance. I love you . . . and I'm ready to face all the . . . problems. If we have to hide for the rest of our lives, we'll hide, that's all. Who knows, maybe someday we won't have to hide anymore, like criminals. It's our life, Serge, yours and mine. We mustn't let other people spoil it.

Silence.

I'd wake up in the morning . . . your place was empty beside me, and I'd tell myself, "This can't go on much longer. I won't be able to stand it."

SERGE:
I know, I couldn't stand it either.

No. 7 Trio

NICOLE:
When your first letter came and you said you were lonely, I think I cried for two days . . .

SERGE:
I wanted to go. I asked for it . . . and God, did I regret it.

LUCIENNE:

> We haven't seen each other for three months and you sit
> there and watch television.

SERGE:

> Why should I tell you about Paris when you've never
> wanted to go there? You can't stand the French.

LUCIENNE:

> That's hardly what I want to talk about . . .

SERGE:

> Your affair doesn't interest me. I've already told you.

LUCIENNE:

> Look, I've thought of something . . .

SERGE:

> No, you're not getting me mixed up in this.

LUCIENNE:

> For Godsake, will you listen to me? . . . You can't go
> on living with Nicole. I mean, you just can't do that,
> people are starting to talk . . . And when I say people, I
> mean the family . . . God forbid anyone else should find
> out. Can you imagine the scandal? . . . Anyway, I was
> thinking . . . Are you listening? Look, either turn off
> that bloody television or I'll smash the thing. Now, if
> I were to get you an apartment somewhere, like near
> Carré St-Louis, for instance? . . . I've seen some nice
> ones there . . . If I were to rent one for you, you'd
> have a nice quiet place to live . . . and every now and
> then you could let us use it, me and Robert . . .

No. 8 Solo

GABRIEL:
> All I ever wanted in my old age is peace and quiet.
> Peace and quiet. Haven't I worked hard enough all my
> life to deserve that? I deserve a peaceful old age.
>
> *Silence.*
>
> I deserve it!
>
> *Silence.*
>
> Excuse me . . .

No. 9 Duet (Trio Finale)

ALBERTINE:
> Your aunt can't take anymore, she just can't. Enough
> is enough . . .

CHARLOTTE:
> You couldn't spare your aunt a couple of dollars, could
> you?

ALBERTINE:
> It's her, I can't take any more of her! Something's
> got to change.

CHARLOTTE:
> Just two dollars, that's all . . .

ALBERTINE:

Stuck in here all day long with . . . with your father whose hearing gets worse every day, and who has no idea what's going on . . . It's not that I don't love him, he's my brother. But he's sick and he won't look after himself . . .

CHARLOTTE:

You see, I haven't received my cheque yet.

ALBERTINE:

And her! Her! One of these days you'll find her with a knife in her back, and you'll know who put it there, too!

CHARLOTTE:

Did she tell you not to give me any money?

ALBERTINE:

Five years, Serge, five years I've been locked in this house with those two!

CHARLOTTE:

Don't listen to her, she tries to make people believe I'm a thief.

ALBERTINE:

For five years I haven't been out of this house, did you know that? It's true! I don't even know where the subway is. I couldn't even find the church on the corner without getting lost. God knows, I'm just as sick as she is, so why is it always me who has to do all the work?

CHARLOTTE:

She doesn't believe I'm sick. She says I'm faking.

ALBERTINE:

To sleep in the same room . . .

CHARLOTTE:

Well, I'm not an actress!

ALBERTINE:

> . . . in the same bed with a sister you'd like to strangle.
> You think that's fun?

CHARLOTTE:

> I wish she was in my shoes. That'd shut her up fast!

ALBERTINE:

> She hogs the whole bed, snores like a cow, gets up fifty
> times a night to pee, coughs and spits for hours on
> end . . .

CHARLOTTE:

> And you know what else she does?

ALBERTINE
AND CHARLOTTE:

> She phones up the whole family to complain about me.

CHARLOTTE:

> I suppose she thinks I don't know, eh? Well, I'm not that
> stupid, no sir. I've got the biggest pension and I give the
> most money, so they'll just have to put up with me.

ALBERTINE:

> She's filthy rich, too. She's rolling in the stuff! She gets
> three cheques at the beginning of each month, and three
> days later there isn't a penny left. She's spent it all on
> pills! Oh, they must love her at the drugstore. She's
> probably keeping them in business. Every year at
> Christmas I expect them to send her a present, for
> Godsake.

CHARLOTTE:

> It's not very nice to say, Serge, but you know, your
> father isn't very nice to Aunt Charlotte either.

ALBERTINE:

> She takes so many pills, sometimes I think she's in
> a coma!

CHARLOTTE:

>He's always taking her side. They're always against me, the two of them. I don't know what she tells him, but I'm the only one he gets mad at. And I never hear them talking. And I should 'cause if you don't shout, he can't understand. If you ask me, she writes to him!

ALBERTINE:

>Sometimes I find her on the floor . . . Yeah, on the floor beside the bed . . . drugged! I can't pick her up, I'm not strong enough. And if your father's off at the tavern, I just leave her there until he gets back. Then she cries and feels sorry for herself, calls me names. But what am I supposed to do? I'm not going to strain my back trying to lift her!

CHARLOTTE:

>Everytime I take a pill I have to double check the bottles to make sure she hasn't switched them on purpose . . .

ALBERTINE:

>You should never have left me alone with them, Serge. When you were here you could talk to them, to her at least. She'll listen to you . . . But me . . .

CHARLOTTE:

>If your aunt promised to give you a little money every month, would you take her to live with you?

ALBERTINE:

>No, things have got to change, Serge. Three sick people alone in one house, it's no good I tell you . . . We can't count on your sisters, they won't have anything to do with us. They treat us like old rags. After all we've done for them . . . But you, I know you wouldn't do that . . . Look, Nicole can manage by herself, she's earning a good salary . . . Why don't you come back?

CHARLOTTE:

I wouldn't take up much room, you know. I wouldn't make any noise.

ALBERTINE:

If you don't come back . . . Well, they're my own flesh and blood, but . . . I might have to leave. I'd feel bad about your father 'cause he can't look after himself and he won't go into a home . . .

CHARLOTTE:

I'd stay out of your way . . . Just a tiny room.

ALBERTINE:

Your room's still there, we never touched it. Aunt Charlotte wanted to take it, but I wouldn't let her . . . 'cause I know you've got a good heart . . .

ALBERTINE
AND CHARLOTTE:

Will you do that for your aunt? Will you?

SERGE:

I'll think about it, okay? I'll think about it.

ALBERTINE:

But you're not saying no?

SERGE:

No.

CHARLOTTE:

When will you give me an answer?

ALBERTINE:

Your aunt will be waiting for an answer . . .

No. 10 Quartet

SERGE:

I never would have thought . . .

LUCIENNE:

What? That I'd stoop so low? Look, if you're going to preach, don't waste your breath. All I'm asking for is a favour, a simple little favour. It's only 'cause I'm sick of looking for new excuses to get out of the house . . .

SERGE:

And paying for hotel rooms . . .

DENISE:

You won't be shocked, will you, if I take a second helping? I mean, you know me, eh? Once a pig always a pig.

LUCIENNE:

Come on. You're always telling me I'm oldfashioned. Between the two of us, I wonder who's worse. You know, I really think . . .

MONIQUE:

Maybe I should take one more pill. I think I'd be okay then . . . Oh don't worry, I won't collapse on you . . . I know when to stop. It's just that I still feel a bit nervous, you know what I mean . . .

DENISE:

For the past few months I've been eating twice what I used to . . . And please, no cracks about my weight, I know I've gotten fatter. In the time you were gone, little brother, your sister Denise went from large to extra large!

MONIQUE:
> Maybe just half a pill . . . that should do it, eh?

LUCIENNE:
> I think that deep down inside you're really shocked.

SERGE:
> I just don't want to be the one who has to come along afterwards and clean up your shit, that's all.

DENISE:
> And the next thing you know . . .

MONIQUE:
> Isn't it clever what they do with these pills? Look, they're all marked . . . So, if you only want to take half a one, or even a quarter . . . Yeah, well, I guess you're not really interested.

LUCIENNE:
> Do you think it's any better, your affair with Nicole?

DENISE: *on the verge of tears*
> Please everyone, just get off my back and let me enjoy my food. That's all I've got left.

No. 11 Solo

LUCIENNE:
> I thought maybe you'd understand . . . After all, your situation isn't exactly normal either, is it? Oh come on, darling, don't look so surprised. We all know. You can cut the innocent lamb routine, we don't buy it anymore. The whole family pretends nothing is wrong, but I wonder what they think when they go to bed at night. No, I saw it all coming for a long time. In fact, I even

talked to Papa about it years ago. Of course, he didn't want to know anything. He pretended he couldn't hear me, as usual. Then Denise and Monique, who thought it was so cute that their little brother and sister should love one another like that. My God! I don't know how many times I told them it wasn't cute at all. It was sick! But did anyone try to stop it? No, they encouraged you, the whole family. You slept in the same room, and in the morning we'd find you in the same bed. Oh that was fine as long as you were kids, but when Nicole got to be fifteen or sixteen, and you ten or eleven, it wasn't so cute anymore, let me tell you. And what did they do? They just closed their eyes and let it go on. Even when they moved, for Godsake, they still let you share the same bedroom. I only started to breathe a little when Nicole left home two years ago . . . I thought it was over, done with. Good Lord, she was twenty-eight and you were twenty-three. It was about time somebody left! But I suppose it was only a lovers quarrel, eh? Or Nicole just went ahead to prepare your little nest, is that it? Last year, when I heard you were moving in with her, that you dared take that out of the house, I was ashamed, Serge, I was so ashamed! You see, what I'm doing, Serge, isn't sick. You're the ones who are sick! Aren't you ashamed when you look each other in the face? Doesn't that bother you? No, I suppose it gets you all excited, eh? Isn't that it, isn't that how you get your kicks?

Silence.

I bet you couldn't even get a hard on for a girl who wasn't your own sister!

No. 12 Solo

NICOLE:

Come over here and sit down . . . It's crazy, but after three months, I feel shy. Like when we were kids and you came back from summer camp . . . You remember? Sometimes it took us a whole week before we could talk to each other.

No. 13 Quintet

LUCIENNE:

You've got nothing to say. You never thought your big sister could figure all that out, eh? Of course not, you always thought the rest of us were idiots.

SERGE:

I'm in love with Nicole and Nicole is in love with me. That's all there is to it.

LUCIENNE:

My God, you can stand there and say it, just like that . . . Could you go and shout it in Papa's ear?

SERGE:

No, I couldn't. But I'd like to. There are so many things I'd like to tell him . . .

DENISE:

Excuse me, eh? It's stupid to cry like that. It doesn't do any good, but . . .

SERGE:

Papa . . .

DENISE:
>Hey, do me a favour and get the pie out of the fridge.

SERGE:
>Papa . . .

DENISE:
>And bring the milk, too.

GABRIEL:
>What?

SERGE:
>If your hearing aid is broken, you tell me, okay?

>*Louder.*

>Your hearing aid . . . If it's not working right, I'll get
>it fixed . . . You've got a guarantee . . .

GABRIEL:
>No, don't bother . . . it's not worth it . . .

SERGE:
>Why, it'd just take a couple of days.

GABRIEL:
>It's not the hearing aid, it's me. It doesn't help me to
>wear it anymore.

CHARLOTTE:
>Yes. I was going to tell you, Serge, but I didn't know
>how . . . Your father went to see the doctor . . .

SERGE:
>Aunt Charlotte, please! Mind your own business!

GABRIEL:
>My headaches kept getting worse, so I went back to
>see them. You know, the one I have here . . . they don't
>make them any stronger. This is the strongest you can

get. That's what they said . . . What can you do? . . .
If I force myself to hear, that's no good either . . . I'm
too old, that's all.

No. 14 Quartet

DENISE: *laughing*

And the next thing you know, I'll be oversize! That's
what I tell myself when I'm face to face with a mincemeat pie. But what can you do, eh? The pie always
wins. I get hypnotized by mincemeat pies. Did you
know that, Serge?

SERGE:

What happened to your diet? You were doing fine when
I left . . .

DENISE:

Stay on a diet when little brother's not around to count
my calories? Are you crazy? Besides, you ought to
know I only went on a diet so you'd come and see me
more often . . . I mean, I made you believe I was on one,
but the minute you went out the door . . .

SERGE:

The mincemeat pie?

DENISE:

The mincemeat pie.

LUCIENNE:

So how much longer is this going to go on? When will
you two get some brains in your heads?

SERGE:

I'm afraid it's going to go on for a long time.

DENISE:

    It's not exactly good for my ulcer, but . . .

SERGE:

    Still scared to have an operation?

DENISE:

    Don't mention that word, I'll be sick to my stomach.
    Oh they say I should have one, but if it's up to me,
    they can bloody well wait till hell freezes over.

LUCIENNE:

    And you can say that without batting an eye? I still
    can't believe it.

SERGE:

    Why? It's simple . . .

DENISE:

    It's simple, the last time I went in all he took was my
    blood pressure and I fell over like a ton of bricks. Crazy,
    eh? If it takes six of them to hold me down just to get
    a blood sample, you can imagine what I'd be like on the
    operating table.

SERGE:

    But after it was over you'd be much better off.

DENISE:

    I wouldn't be better off after because I'd die during.
    I know I would. Come on, let's talk about something
    else. I'm losing my appetite.

MONIQUE:

    I never see him anymore . . .

SERGE:

    Huh? What?

MONIQUE:

> You never listen when I talk to you! I'm talking about Guy. I said I never seen him anymore . . . and I'm fed up. If all he wanted kids for was to dump them in my lap and then beat it, well frankly, he needn't have bothered.

SERGE:

> A salesman has to travel, doesn't he?

MONIQUE:

> Honestly, Serge, you still believe that crap?

SERGE:

> Well, I don't know . . . I hardly know your husband . . . He's always so . . . discreet . . .

MONIQUE:

> Yeah, well that's exactly the point. I've had it with his bloody discretion. Oh sure, he was always around when it was time to have kids. He wouldn't have missed that. But where is he now? Conventions, meetings, God only knows, but he's never at home. Never. And on top of that, he's stuck me with his mother. Well, if that's all my life is, I'd just as soon pull out now. No, I'm sure there's someone else . . . A woman . . . or women . . .

SERGE:

> Don't start that again . . .

No. 15 Solo

MONIQUE:

> What, you too? You're going to tell me I imagine things too? Aren't there enough people doing that already? All day long his mother tells me I imagine things. When he gets home, I can't say two words and he starts screaming I imagine things. Well, I don't imagine things

and I'm sick of being told I do. Five years, five years I've been taking pills on account of my nerves. And for what? To end up listening to that crap? You think that's fun? You think that's any kind of a life? You think I want to end up like Aunt Charlotte, a slave to her bloody tranquilizers? I was really anxious for you to get back . . . I thought you might bring me a little . . . I don't know, a little comfort. But what the hell, I probably shouldn't ask anyone for anything. That's the first thing we should learn in life, not to ask anyone for anything.

No. 16 Quartet

LUCIENNE:
　　And what happens if someone finds out? What's our family going to look like then?

SERGE:
　　It won't look any better if they hear about you.

MONIQUE:
　　I know I'm depressing, but do you think I like that? Do you think I like being the way I am? Look at me, I'm a nervous wreck. If I had a husband who'd look after me I'd be alright, but no, I had to go and marry a Jack-in-the-box! You used to come and see me sometimes and you'd talk to me . . . But now it seems you have nothing more to say . . . You walk in here, you sit down beside me and you stare into the bottom of your coffee cup. Am I really that boring?

SERGE:
　　Sometimes when I come to see you, you're in no shape to talk.

MONIQUE:

Sure, I know, it's all my fault. Look, it's the doctor, our own brother-in-law, who prescribes these pills. What can I do? I have to take them!

DENISE:

If you take the front room like I offered, maybe I'd stick to a diet, a real one . . .

SERGE:

Sure, promises, promises . . .

MONIQUE:

You know, at times I'd like to wash my hands of the whole mess. The house, the kids, the mother-in-law. Wouldn't I love that!

SERGE:

What would you do?

No. 17 Solo

MONIQUE:

I'd come knocking on your door and ask you to take me in, you and Nicole . . . I almost did it when you were away . . . In fact, I did do it . . . I got up right in the middle of Carol Burnett and I went to see Nicole. She'll tell you all about it when you see her . . . I spent the night at your place and then in the morning I came home. Or, to be more precise, I got kicked out. Oh, Nicole was very polite about it, you know how she is . . . She tried to convince me that my duty was here, but I know she didn't believe a word of it . . . I guess she just didn't know how to get rid of me . . . Jesus! Another one . . . Oh well, what's the difference. I didn't sleep that night anyway 'cause I'd gone out of the house without my stupid pills.

No. 18 Trio

DENISE: *laughing*

Why should one sister have you all to herself, eh?
What about the other three? There's at least one who's
very plump and very tasty who'd be willing to do a lot
for you . . .

SERGE:

I had enough of being passed around when I was a kid.
I'll decide for myself, thanks.

LUCIENNE:

Too bad, kiddo, you won't get off that easy.

SERGE:

Denise, please, no tickling! I'm not a baby anymore.

DENISE:

For crying out loud, I haven't seen you for three
months. Let me have some fun, will you?

SERGE:

Cut it out or I'll leave!

DENISE:

Good Lord, aren't we getting stuck up! Is that what
they teach you in Europe? Okay, I get the message. From
now on I'll admire you from a distance. Just give me
your picture and I'll set it on the TV . . . Good Lord!

LUCIENNE:

Look, I'm the oldest, so I'm responsible.

SERGE:

So what are you going to do, tell Papa? It'll kill him
and you know it.

LUCIENNE:
And what if he finds out from somebody else?

SERGE:
He won't find out if you keep your mouth shut. Just leave him alone, that's all he wants. And stop trying to get back at me because I won't run your whore house.

DENISE:
If I want to see you in person, I'll send you an engraved invitation imploring you to come.

SERGE:
Denise, you're a drag.

DENISE:
M-m-m-m . . . You're so handsome when you're angry. You make my armpits bristle with excitement!

SERGE: *laughing*
Come on, quit horsing around. We're not kids anymore.

DENISE:
A kiss, a kiss, a kiss . . .

SERGE:
Hey, that tickles, cut it out.

DENISE:
I'd forgotten how good you smell. Oh God, I think I'm going to faint.

SERGE:
I'm leaving . . .

DENISE:
Surrender! Surrender! Hey, let's play hide and seek. You hide.

SERGE:
>   Come on, this is ridiculous. We're acting like a couple
>   of idiots.

DENISE:
>   No one can see us.

SERGE:
>   Denise!

DENISE:
>   Okay, okay. Back to the mincemeat pie.

SERGE:
>   Whew! . . . I'm so warm . . . You really scare me some-
>   times, you know that?

DENISE:
>   Oh, come on. It's only a joke . . .

No. 19 Quartet

NICOLE:
>   You look exhausted . . . we ought to go to bed.

DENISE:
>   It's only a joke . . .

MONIQUE:
>   Hey, my head's spinning all of a sudden . . . Maybe the
>   pills are too strong . . .

LUCIENNE:
>   I won't say anything to Papa . . . But Denise and
>   Monique aren't going to like it, not one little bit.

No. 20 Trio

GABRIEL:
Serge . . . There's something I want to tell you . . .

ALBERTINE:
I'm sick of watching television day in day out . . .

GABRIEL:
We never had a good talk, you and me . . .

ALBERTINE:
It's always the same . . .

GABRIEL:
I can't hear . . . besides, I was always too embarrassed . . .

CHARLOTTE:
I can hardly stand up anymore, but no one ever believes me . . .

GABRIEL:
Down at the tavern I'm always solving the world's problems, but when it comes to my own kids . . . that takes . . . I don't know . . . just something I never had . . .

ALBERTINE:
Always the same . . .

GABRIEL:
I guess I was never brought up that way . . .

ALBERTINE:
Always the same . . .

GABRIEL:
I always felt kind of awkward with you kids, and maybe I made you the same way . . .

ALBERTINE:
> Even their movies are boring. I've seen them all.

GABRIEL:
> But there's something I have to tell you . . .

CHARLOTTE:
> They want to kill me to get my insurance . . .

GABRIEL:
> Even if it's kind of hard . . .

CHARLOTTE:
> That's what they're after . . .

GABRIEL:
> There's something . . . I want to thank you for . . .

CHARLOTTE:
> It's true, your aunt knows it!

GABRIEL:
> I wanted to tell you before you left, but I wasn't able
> to . . .

CHARLOTTE:
> Well, they won't get me that easy . . .

GABRIEL:
> And it's taking about all I've got to tell you now . . .

ALBERTINE:
> There isn't a movie I haven't seen. There's never
> anything new . . .

GABRIEL:
> You remember when you all got together to buy me my
> first hearing aid . . .

ALBERTINE:

I watch the dumb thing from ten in the morning right through til midnight.

GABRIEL:

That was seven or eight years ago . . .

ALBERTINE:

No wonder I've seen everything . . .

GABRIEL:

I never said anything, I was too proud . . .

CHARLOTTE:

I'll bury them all.

GABRIEL:

But after I turned sixty and was getting close to retirement . . . and then when I lost my job, I finally gave in. I said to myself, all I have left in my life is to try and hear other people . . .

CHARLOTTE:

They laugh at me now, but you wait. I'll bury them all, one after the other . . .

GABRIEL:

Well . . . I don't know how to describe it, but . . .

ALBERTINE:

There are too many comedy shows, I don't like that either.

GABRIEL:

But the day I got my hearing aid I was scared at first. It was giving me a terrible headache 'cause I'd hardly heard a thing for forty years . . .

ALBERTINE:

They don't make me laugh, those things . . .

GABRIEL:
Just the sirens going by, or the vibrations in the floor . . .

ALBERTINE:
They're not the least bit funny . . .

GABRIEL:
Then, when I came back to the house . . . and I heard your voices, you can't imagine what that did to me . . .

CHARLOTTE:
All Aunt Bartine ever does is say bad things about me . . . But God's going to punish her.

GABRIEL:
I didn't know the sound of your voices, my own kids . . .

CHARLOTTE:
And the day I find her lying on the floor, I won't lift a finger . . .

GABRIEL:
It was the first time in my life I'd heard you speak . . .

CHARLOTTE:
She'll find out what it's like . . .

GABRIEL:
Maybe you don't know it, Serge, but that afternoon you gave me the most beautiful present . . .

CHARLOTTE:
I'll leave her there to die.

GABRIEL:
You don't remember what you did?

CHARLOTTE:
Too bad for her.

GABRIEL:
Nicole had just bought that new stereo . . .

ALBERTINE:
It's like the commercials . . .

GABRIEL:
. . . and you took me into the parlour, and you sat me down in my chair . . .

ALBERTINE:
They try to make us believe all kinds of nonsense . . .

GABRIEL:
. . . and you said . . .

ALBERTINE:
They think we're stupid . . .

GABRIEL:
"Listen to this, Papa!"

ALBERTINE:
They can't fool me. I know it's all lies . . .

GABRIEL:
Then you put on a record . . .

CHARLOTTE:
I can't wait to see her die.

GABRIEL:
I don't remember what it was, I don't know music, but . . .

CHARLOTTE:
And the rest of them with her.

GABRIEL:
. . . for forty years, Serge, I hadn't heard any music.

ALBERTINE:

> Oh, Charlotte, stop criticizing!

GABRIEL:

> All I ever heard was the loud parts, the fanfares . . . But then . . .

CHARLOTTE:

> And what about you with your bloody complaints?

GABRIEL:

> To hear the violins, Serge, to hear the violins . . . It was like I was in Heaven . . . Goddamn it, like I was in Heaven!

CHARLOTTE:

> I long for the day when your mouth will be shut for good.

GABRIEL:

> It was the most beautiful present . . . the most beautiful present in my whole life . . .

ALBERTINE:

> And how about me? Don't think I'm not sick of listening to you. There are times I wish I was deaf.

GABRIEL:

> Now you can say . . . for once in his life, your old man's had a talk with you.

No. 21 Quartet

NICOLE:
> Why don't you take a shower before you go to bed?
> You'll feel better . . .

MONIQUE:
> Maybe I'd feel better if I lay down for a bit . . . Come
> on, let's go into the bedroom . . .

NICOLE:
> Get some sleep. We'll talk about it again in the morning
> . . . I mean, we haven't talked about it at all, but we'll
> try in the morning. I told them at the office I wouldn't
> be in.

MONIQUE:
> When you're here, it doesn't seem so bad . . . I think I
> even breathe better . . . It's so warm in here . . . Why
> don't you take off your shirt . . .

DENISE:
> There are some things you've got to understand, eh? . . .
> If I joke with you like this . . .

LUCIENNE:
> You were so good then, Serge, so good . . .

MONIQUE:
> You can take your shirt off . . . You're not embarrassed
> in front of me, are you?

LUCIENNE:
> I mean, when you were little, you'd listen to me . . .

MONIQUE
AND LUCIENNE:
> I saw you come into the world. I watched you grow
> up . . .

DENISE:

> You know how I love to have fun . . . But lately, whenever I open my mouth . . .

LUCIENNE:

> Remember? . . . You'd do whatever I wanted . . .

MONIQUE:

> Don't worry, I'm not going to rape you . . .

DENISE:

> You're the only one who isn't ashamed of me . . .

LUCIENNE:

> Sometimes you'd call me your second mama . . . Of course Mama didn't like that, but still, it was partly true . . .

MONIQUE:

> I just want to look at you . . . Didn't you ever notice how I'd look at you when we'd go swimming in the summer with the kids?

DENISE:

> It's at the point . . .

MONIQUE:

> It doesn't hurt to look . . .

DENISE:

> It's at the point now . . .

MONIQUE:

> And you're a lot more exciting to look at than my bag-of-bones husband . . .

DENISE:

> It's at the point now where even Gaston is ashamed of me.

MONIQUE:

> We haven't seen each other for three months. Surely
> you could do me this one little favour?

DENISE:

> I mean, seriously, can you believe it? They say I'm
> vulgar!

LUCIENNE:

> Your second Mama, eh? Remember that?

MONIQUE:

> Remember when you were little and I used to give you
> your bath? You remember? It was always me who gave
> you your bath. Denise would take you out, Lucienne
> would buy you clothes and stuff you full of chocolate,
> then I got to wash you. And Nicole . . . Nicole was
> forever throwing fits because we'd take away her darling
> little brother. She was so cute though . . . Hey, you
> remember when I'd give you your baths together?

LUCIENNE:

> I was the one who really brought you up, not Mama.
> I was already twenty by the time you were born. It was
> me who bought all your clothes . . . With my own
> money too. And boy, did you look smart.

MONIQUE:

> There was no hot water in those days. We'd get a big
> kettle boiling on the stove and pour it into the cold
> bath . . . I'd undress you, you and Nicole, then I'd put
> you both in the tub . . . and I'd scrub like crazy . . .
> especially you! . . .

LUCIENNE:

> You remember the white woollen pants you used to
> wear? You were the only kid on the block with a pair
> like that . . .

DENISE:

    Used to be everyone thought I was funny. Remember when you were a kid? Boy, you thought I was a riot.

MONIQUE:

    And boy, did you ever like to get scrubbed.

LUCIENNE:

    And I bought baby blue jerseys to go with them.

DENISE:

    Of course I gotta admit, I'd do anything to make you laugh.

LUCIENNE:

    Remember that? You'd walk around stiff as a board.

MONIQUE:

    You'd squirm like a fish . . . a slippery little fish.

NICOLE:

    I had it all worked out in my head, everything I wanted to say . . .

MONIQUE:

    That's what I used to call you . . .

LUCIENNE:

    I used to call you my little soldier. You were already proud as hell, even then . . .

DENISE:

    Remember when I used to read you "Little Red Riding Hood?"

NICOLE:

    But now . . .

DENISE:

    And I'd take out my two front teeth and say, "The better to eat you with, my dear."

NICOLE:

>I don't want to talk. I just want to look at you.

DENISE:

>Then you'd stop laughing, eh? . . . You were scared out of your wits!

LUCIENNE:

>You knew you were good looking, didn't you? And you know you still are. Come on, say it.

DENISE:

>And I loved to scare you, 'cause then I'd get to grab you all over.

NICOLE:

>I don't know what to do. I'm so happy you're here, then all of a sudden . . .

LUCIENNE:

>Say it.

NICOLE:

>My old fears come back . . . I have the feeling I played with you too much . . . I know we said we wouldn't talk about that anymore . . . but . . . I don't want you to feel like a kid with his mother . . .

LUCIENNE:

>You're not as well dressed now as you used to be, that's for sure.

MONIQUE:

>It scares me . . . the way . . . I fall asleep like that . . . It's weird . . .

NICOLE:

>Even if it's not my fault . . .

DENISE:

> I'd wait for my turn to babysit, then I'd really scare you. Papa went out on Saturday nights, so we all took turns looking after you. We each got to keep you, one night a month, and did we take advantage of that!

MONIQUE:

> I wish you'd take off your . . .

DENISE:

> When my turn came, you were petrified 'cause you knew I'd hide on you or tell you scary stories . . .

MONIQUE:

> Why don't you . . . lie down . . . next to me?

NICOLE:

> Honestly, Serge, I never saw this coming!

DENISE:

> But you loved it, I know you did.

LUCIENNE:

> The money I spent on you!

DENISE:

> You loved every minute of it, didn't you?

LUCIENNE:

> You're first long pants . . . your first record-player . . . Hey, that's right, I'd forgotten about that. I didn't have a cent to my name, but I bought you your first record-player.

DENISE:

> But now . . .

NICOLE:

> And I didn't want it to happen!

DENISE:
>I'll have to be satisfied just looking at you.

NICOLE:
>It's not our fault, Serge, I know it's not. It's their fault.
>They're the ones to blame.

LUCIENNE:
>You never thought of that, did you, darling? You still
>have a few debts to pay.

DENISE: *very slowly*
>"The better to eat you with, you little son-of-a-bitch."
>And I'd bite you all over.

No. 22 Solo

DENISE:
>But now when I try to be funny, you're the only one
>who laughs . . . It's true . . . You know, we've had the
>store for five years now . . . We worked hard to get that
>place, Gaston and I . . . And we were happy too . . . Me,
>I worked the cash, so we'd save a salary and . . .
>
>*Near tears.*
>
>Gaston doesn't want me at the cash anymore because he
>thinks I'm too fat! He's ashamed of me . . . He . . . He
>. . . He gets upset when I'm around! Oh, he hasn't said
>so himself, but I can tell, I'm not blind. You know me,
>I like to joke with the customers, eh? I like to laugh . . .
>and . . . Okay, so I always talk about my weight, but
>what do you expect? I'd rather laugh at myself in front
>of people than have them laugh behind my back. But
>Gaston doesn't like it anymore. He gets all in a huff the
>minute I crack a joke. I don't know how to explain it
>to you because I don't understand it myself. I'm so

worried, I'm so confused, I feel like I'm going crazy. Before, when I'd clown around, he'd be the first to laugh. And he married me 'cause he liked plump women, for Godsake, so what's come over him all of a sudden? Maybe I go too far with my jokes, maybe that's it.

Trying to laugh.

I don't know. I think it's fun telling dirty jokes to all those prudes and old ladies. Gaston must be afraid of losing customers . . . No . . . No, it's not that. He's ashamed of me, I know it. He's ashamed of me 'cause I'm too fat! Well at least you don't mind, eh, Serge? You don't mind if I'm fat, do you?

No. 23 Solo

SERGE:
You're not fat, Denise. How many times do I have to tell you? It's all in your head. You're the one who keeps saying you're fat. Nobody else thinks so. If you'd only stop talking about it, stop making it the centre of your life. It's all in your head, Denise. You're not fat . . . You're just . . . well, a bit chunky maybe.

No. 24 Solo

LUCIENNE: *slowly*
All I'd have to do is pick up the phone . . . Can't you just see the look on their faces? Monique, of course would swallow a whole bottle of pills . . . And Denise . . . well, when things go badly for Denise, there's always the fridge . . . So, that would make it "official"

for all four of us . . . I wonder whether we'd talk about it amongst ourselves or if we'd still try to keep it hidden . . . One thing's for sure, family get-togethers would never be the same . . . I can see it now. Being in that house would be like sitting on a powder keg. Silences so thick you could cut them with a knife. You're right though, I won't do it. There are enough traumas in this family already. I'm the oldest, the most responsible, so I'll go on filling Mama's shoes. Someone's got to do it. Remember what I told you before you left? Maybe I had to get drunk to say it, but I'm glad I did 'cause I haven't changed my mind.

Laughing.

It's true, Serge. My god, it's true. You should have been a queer!

No. 25 Duet

LUCIENNE:
You can't imagine how I've wanted that to happen. You can't imagine. For years I've known that's the best thing that could happen to you.

NICOLE:
When it happened . . . When I first realized that when you were with me, it wasn't my little brother anymore . . . it was a guy, almost a man . . . and that you were looking at me the way a man looks at a woman . . . I got so scared. I didn't want it to happen Serge! I didn't want it!

LUCIENNE:
We used you like a toy in that house. We played with you, we fussed over you, we brought you up like a little girl, or rather like a kid who had no sex. I could

see what would happen . . . With all those women
around, you'd get screwed up. You'd turn against them
and you'd . . .

NICOLE:

Before that, I never thought it was serious. We were just
kids . . . we were just playing. And everyone else, they
thought it was so cute . . . I was just playing with you
like a kid, that's all!

LUCIENNE: *bursts out laughing*

You know what, Serge? That was your only escape and
you didn't take it . . . So all I can say is, too bad for
you. That's it, just too bad for you.

NICOLE:

The first time when you came to me on the sofa and it
wasn't just to kiss me good night . . . You were so
beautiful, Serge!

LUCIENNE:

'Cause, believe me, you'd be better off with another
guy than with your own sister.

NICOLE:

I'd been dreaming about it for a long time, though I'd
never admitted it to myself . . . But when it happened
. . . it was so frightening and so beautiful . . . that I
wished . . . I wished we could both die right there so no
one would ever know, ever . . . And mostly so I wouldn't
have to remember . . .

LUCIENNE:

I told your friend Robert all about it. Oh, we had a
wonderful time!

NICOLE:

But the next morning we were both alive and things
kept going on as usual. I didn't even feel guilty. You
were so happy . . . and so was I.

LUCIENNE:

You know, Robert and I feel the same way about this. He also thinks you're kind of sick.

NICOLE:

Then the second time . . . I didn't think it was ugly or frightening . . . It just made me happy, that's all . . . 'cause it was only natural that it should happen, I guess . . .

LUCIENNE:

Well, as my husband would say, if I could choose my diseases, I'd take the other one. At least that way I wouldn't be so ashamed of you.

NICOLE:

And . . . it was beautiful.

No. 26 Solo

SERGE:

Poor Lucienne, you seem to think you're the only one in the family with brains. Why do you think I took off for three months? For a vacation? Not with the job I've got. Christ, I had to borrow money to leave because, believe it or not, this has also created some big problems for Nicole and me. You see, we've also needed to think about things. Don't forget, I haven't had much choice in all this. After all, it was the rest of you who pushed me into it, not realizing, at least I hope not realizing, what the hell you were doing. So, here I am in the arms of Nicole and she's thirty and I'm twenty-five. So you can well imagine I've been asking myself some pretty hard questions. Okay, I'm with Nicole now, but is that really what I want? Am I happy with Nicole? Well, Lucienne, after three months without her, I can tell you yes, I am happy with Nicole and yes, I'm going to stay with her.

I don't care if you're ashamed of me or not. I don't care if we have to move far away, we're together, Lucienne, and we're going to stay that way for as long as we possibly can. It's clear, it's simple, and I know what I'm doing. What I feel for Nicole and what Nicole feels for me is love, Lucienne. It's love and it's real. It's not a matter of protection or security, it's love. And it's beautiful. So don't let anyone tell me I don't have the right, because I do have the right. I have the right to be happy like anyone else and I'm lucky because I've found my happiness. Maybe I've found it in my own sister, but I'm through being ashamed of it. And if the rest of you lead shitty lives with your shitty husbands at least have some respect for us, because we're happy. We're going to live, Lucienne, we're going to help each other live. And how's this for beautiful? We're going to live together without hurting one another . . . I explained all this in my letters to Nicole and now I can't wait to see her so I can tell her face to face. And one other thing . . . Don't bother telling Robert about this, I'll tell him myself . . . And I bet he'll stop laughing even if you don't.

No. 27 Solo

NICOLE:

Before I got your first letter, I started to think you'd forgotten me. Stupid, eh? I told myself maybe we were right to separate. Maybe now that he's there he's realized he's better off without me. Maybe after tasting a bit of . . . freedom . . . well, maybe he doesn't want to come back . . . It's crazy the stuff you imagine when you're waiting to hear from someone. A month is a long time. A whole month without any sign of life from my . . . And me, I'd promised you I wouldn't write first, that I'd wait, so . . . by the time your letter came I'd almost given up hope . . . I came home for lunch one day . . . You wouldn't believe how I cried, Serge. I must have looked like one of those crazy French movies we're always laughing at on TV. You know the ones, when the girl finally gets a letter from her lover, she either goes charging all over the house or she throws herself on the bed, beating her breast, bawling her eyes out . . . Well, I did all of that. I did. I was so happy to finally hear from my . . . lover . . . And not only that, but you said you were lonely. And that you loved me. And you said it was going to be tough, but that you'd stick it out for the three months. I'm glad you stayed the three months. This way we know for sure . . . I phoned home right away to tell them I'd heard from you . . . All Aunt Charlotte said was that they'd had a telegram from you when you arrived in Paris, they hadn't heard a word since, that Papa was worried about you . . . and then she hung up. Serge, we've got to do something about Papa. If he's alone with those two much longer, they're going to drive him crazy. Now, I had an idea . . . If you don't like it we won't do it . . . but listen . . .

No. 28 Trio

ALBERTINE:
It gets to the point you don't know what to do anymore . . .

SERGE: *very loudly*
Papa . . .

ALBERTINE:
Roast beef one day . . .

SERGE:
Can you hear me, Papa?

ALBERTINE:
> Chicken or spaghetti the next . . .

SERGE:
> I thought about you a lot while I was away . . .

ALBERTINE:
> Then a roast of veal or maybe a stew . . .

SERGE:
> Papa, not once in our lives have we had a serious conversation.

ALBERTINE:
> And then, you're stuck. You don't know what to do anymore.

SERGE:
> I hardly know you. And I'm sure you hardly know me.

ALBERTINE:
> So you go back and start over . . .

SERGE:
> When I was a kid, I never saw you 'cause you worked nights, and then later . . .

CHARLOTTE:
> Your aunt is sick of eating the same old thing . . .

SERGE:
> Ever since Mama died, you've been escaping to the tavern . . .

CHARLOTTE:
> When it comes to cooking, Aunt Bartine's got no imagination . . .

SERGE:
> I don't even know who you are! You never told us!

CHARLOTTE:
I know everything costs a lot . . .

SERGE:
Even if your hearing was bad, there were times when I
needed to talk to you . . . We were the only two men
in the house.

ALBERTINE:
But Good Lord, everything costs a fortune . . .

SERGE:
I remember when I was in school. Sometimes I'd write
you letters when I needed your advice, but then I'd
throw them away 'cause I was too embarrassed to give
them to you . . .

ALBERTINE:
We have a hard time making ends meet, so I can't always
fix what I'd like . . .

SERGE:
How come everyone was always so embarrassed in this
house?

CHARLOTTE:
Even if we spent a fortune on food, she'd waste it . . .

SERGE:
I mean, we could have learned to use signs or something.

ALBERTINE:
Of course, your aunt's had an awful time with her
arthritis . . .

SERGE:
Once again, Papa, I have to shout things we'd normally
whisper . . . and it's difficult.

ALBERTINE:
Your poor aunt can't even make a pie crust anymore . . .

SERGE:

I thought about you a lot while I was gone and I realized something terrible . . .

ALBERTINE:

Say what you will, those ready-made pie crusts aren't nearly as good . . .

SERGE:

You've never heard us say that we love you!

ALBERTINE:

They're like candy . . .

SERGE:

I know it bothers you . . . Don't turn away . . .

ALBERTINE:

Nothing but sugar and air.

SERGE:

Look at me . . .

CHARLOTTE:

Your aunt tried to bake you a cake to celebrate your coming home . . .

SERGE:

I know, you think men don't say these things to each other . . .

CHARLOTTE:

But I wish you could have seen it . . . We had to throw it away . . .

SERGE:

I love you, Papa!

CHARLOTTE:

Hard as a rock!

SERGE:

I may be twenty years too late, I'm no longer a kid, but I still need to say it. I love you!

ALBERTINE:

And your father, he hardly eats a thing these days.

SERGE:

Even if you don't hear, that's no reason not to tell you these things.

ALBERTINE:

He pokes around in his plate a little, but he leaves everything . . .

SERGE:

You can at least read my lips. Papa, I love you!

CHARLOTTE:

She gives him the best parts and he doesn't even touch them!

SERGE:

And if nobody's told you that for forty years 'cause it's the sort of thing you don't shout, well, too bad, I'll shout it. Papa, I love you!

CHARLOTTE:

All I get are the scraps . . .

SERGE:

Because I know you need that, you too.

ALBERTINE:

It's not even worth trying anymore.

SERGE:

Don't cry.

ALBERTINE:

It's not worth it . . .

SERGE:
Papa, please don't cry.

ALBERTINE:
It's not worth the effort . . .

SERGE:
Don't cry . . .

ALBERTINE:
It's too late to make the effort. It's too late.

No. 29 Octet

NICOLE:
I know it sounds cruel, but what else can we do? We can't leave him there. The others can't take him, they all have families. And with us, well . . . it wouldn't be long before he realized . . . So I thought maybe . . . if we all got together . . . perhaps we could put him in a home . . .

SERGE:
Never! Absolutely never!

NICOLE:
Some of them are okay, you know.

SERGE:
Don't ever mention that again, Nicole. Never!

MONIQUE:
Hey, did I fall asleep? I must have . . . God, these pills are strong. How long did I sleep?

SERGE:
Ten minutes . . . No longer.

MONIQUE:
> You must help me to relax 'cause I feel wonderful . . .
> I think I even had a dream . . . I haven't had a dream for
> months. Hey, don't go away. You're good for my
> nerves . . .

SERGE:
> No, I'm afraid I have to go now . . .

NICOLE:
> Do you want him to stay there?

SERGE:
> No, I know he's got to get out of there . . . I never
> realized it so much as tonight . . . But look, Denise has
> a parlour that's empty . . . she just offered it to me . . .
> She could take Papa . . . And things aren't too hot with
> Lucienne and her husband so she wants to find an
> apartment . . . And Monique wants to get out of her
> place . . . I want Papa out of there, Nicole, but he's not
> going into a home. That would kill him.

GABRIEL:
> Go on home, Serge, go home and get some sleep . . .
> You must be half dead . . .

> *Very long silence.*

SERGE:
> Okay, I guess I'll be on my way . . .

GABRIEL:
> Come and see us more often . . .

ALBERTINE
AND CHARLOTTE:
> Your aunt gets lonesome . . .

DENISE:
> So soon? Come and see me more often . . .

ALBERTINE
AND CHARLOTTE:
> All by herself, day after day . . . with her!

MONIQUE:
> You'll come see me more often, won't you?

GABRIEL:
> I mean, when you feel like it. Don't think you have to.

DENISE:
> It's so nice for me . . .

MONIQUE:
> It's so good for me . . .

NICOLE:
> But what do we do with the aunts?

LUCIENNE:
> Serge . . .

DENISE:
> And think about my offer, eh? I'm serious . . .

LUCIENNE:
> Even if we've argued a bit . . . think about what I said . . .

MONIQUE:
> And if ever you find me on your doorstep, don't send
> me away . . .

NICOLE:
> They've looked after him for ten years, we can't just
> abandon them . . . It's true though, they have kids of
> their own . . . Why can't they take care of them?

GABRIEL:
> And bring me some more books . . . I read all that stuff
> you gave me before you left . . . The days are kind of
> long . . . That's why I go down to the tavern so often . . .

NICOLE:
>Let's go to bed . . . Come on, we'll talk about it in the morning. You look like you're ready to drop . . .

LUCIENNE:
>Serge . . . Before you go . . . I've thought of something else . . .

>*Very long silence.*

>You could take Papa with you . . .

>*Very fast.*

>If you agree, we'll get a big apartment and give Papa a room of his own. He'd be better off with you than with those two hags . . . Then . . . Robert could pretend to come and see you . . . and me too . . .

MONIQUE:
>Goodbye, sweetie . . .

DENISE:
>See you, sexy . . .

LUCIENNE:
>Think about it . . .

SERGE:
>Nicole . . . If all else fails . . . Lucienne had a suggestion . . .

GABRIEL:
>Hey, I forgot to tell you . . . You know Bonnier, my buddy down at the tavern? Well, he's got a sister, and she saw you in Paris.

ALBERTINE:
>Button up good and warm now. Don't let your neck get cold.

MONIQUE:
>Wrap up warmly . . .

DENISE:
>Come on, put your scarf on . . .

LUCIENNE:
>Put up your collar . . .

ALL THE WOMEN
EXCEPT NICOLE:
>You'll freeze to death!

GABRIEL:
>She tried to say hello to you, but you were walking and
>she was riding in a tourist bus.

CHARLOTTE:
>Can you loan me the two dollars?

GABRIEL:
>She's sure it was you though . . . She wished she could
>have talked to you, but . . .

ALBERTINE:
>Phone me during the week . . .

CHARLOTTE:
>Your aunt really needs it ... .

GABRIEL:
>I mean, she never thought she'd run into someone she
>knew in Paris!

>*Very long silence.*

MONIQUE:
>Goodbye.

DENISE:
>See you.

LUCIENNE:
> So long.

NICOLE:
> Good night.

SERGE:
> Well . . . My taxi . . . My taxi's here . . .

ALL EXCEPT
SERGE AND NICOLE:
> Bonjour, là! Bonjour!

No. 30 Octet

Very rapid

Long and insistent doorbell.

ALBERTINE:
> My God, you scared me half to death!

CHARLOTTE:
> I thought it was the phone ringing . . .

ALBERTINE:
> Is something the matter?

CHARLOTTE:
> I stood there like a donkey yelling into the receiver.

SERGE:
> Is Papa asleep?

ALBERTINE:
> It's two o'clock in the morning!

SERGE:
> I want to talk to him . . .

CHARLOTTE:
> That's ridiculous. Come back tomorrow.

SERGE:
> I want to talk to him now!

ALBERTINE:
> Are you crazy barging in here at this hour?

CHARLOTTE:
> Is somebody sick?

ALBERTINE:
> It's Nicole! Is Nicole sick?

CHARLOTTE:
> Why didn't you phone? That would have been faster.

GABRIEL:
> What's going on out here? The whole house is shaking. What are you doing here at this hour?

CHARLOTTE:
> Nicole is sick . . .

GABRIEL:
> What?

ALBERTINE: *louder*
> Nicole is very sick!

CHARLOTTE:
> Nicole is sick . . .

SERGE:
> Nicole is not sick . . . Nobody's sick!

ALBERTINE:
> But you just said . . .

SERGE:
> I just said I wanted to talk to my father. You're the ones who . . .

GABRIEL:
> What's going on? I can't hear a thing. Speak up!

SERGE:
> I want to talk to you.

GABRIEL:
> At three o'clock in the morning?

CHARLOTTE:
> No, it's only two . . .

GABRIEL:
> Can't it wait till tomorrow?

SERGE:
> No.

> *Louder.*

> No, I've got to talk to you right away. Otherwise, I might change my mind . . .

MONIQUE:
> Hello, Denise, wait till you hear what's happened!

GABRIEL:
> What do you mean, change your mind?

ALBERTINE:
> Are you coming home to stay like I asked?

DENISE:
> Eh? What? What's happened? What time is it?

SERGE:
>   Papa, I'm going to make you an offer and I want an answer right now.

MONIQUE:
>   Lucienne just phoned . . . You won't believe this . . .

CHARLOTTE:
>   An offer?

GABRIEL:
>   What do you mean, an offer?

SERGE: *almost screaming*
>   Nicole and I want you to come and live with us!

ALBERTINE:
>   Serge!

CHARLOTTE:
>   Dear God!

LUCIENNE:
>   Hello, Nicole? Are you happy now? You've won it all, eh? Right down the line!

MONIQUE:
>   Papa's moving in with Serge and Nicole.

GABRIEL:
>   Couldn't you have waited till morning to ask me that?

DENISE:
>   But that's crazy. Serge is supposed to move in with us.

SERGE:
>   I want an answer now! I don't want you to stay here any longer.

ALBERTINE:
>   Sure. Come right out and say it. We torture him!

LUCIENNE:
    The least you can do is answer me.

CHARLOTTE:
    Is this all the thanks we get for looking after him?

NICOLE:
    Lucienne, I've nothing to say to you.

DENISE:
    When is he going to move?

NICOLE:
    Nothing at all.

MONIQUE:
    As soon as possible I guess.

ALBERTINE:
    You're abandonning us!

CHARLOTTE:
    You bastard!

NICOLE:
    Wait, Lucienne. There is one thing . . . Papa's going to
    be fine with us. We'll take good care of him . . .

LUCIENNE:
    Filthy pigs!

MONIQUE:
    And do you know what else she tried to make me
    believe?

NICOLE:
    Sure, that's it. Good night . . .

MONIQUE:
    But it can't be true. It's disgusting!

DENISE:

Coming from her, I'm not surprised. Don't worry, don't believe a word she says . . .

ALBERTINE:

What's going to happen to us?

CHARLOTTE:

You never thought of that, did you? That's not your problem. You couldn't care less!

SERGE:

Will you shut up!

Silence.

I'm sorry. I didn't mean to say that . . . But I've got to talk to my father . . . I know you'll listen anyway, but please go back to your room. This is between me and him. I don't want you butting in.

ALBERTINE:

Come on, Charlotte.

CHARLOTTE:

We know when we're not wanted.

DENISE:

You'll never get me to believe that, Monique. And you ought to be ashamed of yourself for even thinking it.

MONIQUE:

Yes, but if she took the trouble to phone me in the middle of the night . . .

DENISE:

Goodbye!

MONIQUE:

Hello? Hello?

No. 31 Final Duet

GABRIEL:

    Sit down . . . Sit down on the bed . . . You still don't smoke?

SERGE:

    No.

GABRIEL:

    That's about my fourth cigarette tonight . . .

SERGE:

    One of these days you're going to burn the house down . . .

GABRIEL:

    If it hasn't happened yet, it never will . . .

SERGE:

    Yeah, sure.

GABRIEL:

    Have you . . . thought about what you're asking me?

SERGE:

    No.

GABRIEL:

    The consequences . . .

SERGE:

    I don't care about that . . .

GABRIEL:

    Your two aunts . . .

SERGE:

    They've got their own families . . .

GABRIEL:

> And I've got my habits . . . I'm seventy years old . . .

SERGE:

> Nothing will have to change, Papa. We don't live far
> away . . . You won't even have to change neighbour-
> hoods . . .

GABRIEL:

> I'm not much good around the house, you know . . .

SERGE:

> Don't worry about that. That'll work itself out. The
> important thing is for you to get out of here and fast.

GABRIEL:

> You're putting quite a load on your shoulders . . .

SERGE:

> No, I'm not . . .

> *Silence.*

GABRIEL:

> Serge . . .

SERGE:

> Yeah?

GABRIEL:

> Serge, if you only knew . . . how long I've waited for
> this . . . for one of my kids . . .

SERGE:

> So your answer is yes?

GABRIEL:

> I'll think about it . . . I really will.

SERGE:

Papa . . . There's one other thing . . . It's serious, very serious . . .

GABRIEL:

Don't bother about that. I know about that.

SERGE:

You know about it? For how long?

GABRIEL:

For a long time. But we won't talk about it now. Your two aunts are listening. Go on home now . . . Go to bed . . .

SERGE:

Yeah, okay. Bonjour là.

GABRIEL:

Bonjour.

Fade.